Grace vs Works

Pastor
Harold Adam Arrington

Unless otherwise indicated, Scriptures and quotations are from the King James Version of the Holy Bible.

Sugarcane Publishing

ISBN-10: 0692669795
ISBN-13: 978-0692669792

IN JESUS' NAME?

Exposed: The "Jesus Only" Doctrine
- A Body of Belief Contrary to the Cross of
Calvary -

By Rev. Harold Adam Arrington

A Handbook for Every Christian

A discussion of **Three Critical Errors** in the
"Jesus Only" doctrine, and a defense of Christianity against all works-related doctrinal beliefs.

TABLE OF CONTENTS

Acknowledgements
Preface

PART I: WATER BAPTISM

PART II: THE TRINITY

PART III – WORKS OF RIGHTEOUSNESS

ABOUT THE AUTHOR

ACKNOWLEDGEMENTS

With love, to my darling wife Barbara, my six sons, three daughters and their spouses, my grandchildren, great-grandchildren, and my entire Bethel Gospel Tabernacle Family.

PREFACE

The purpose of this book is to inform, instruct, and illuminate the truth of the Gospel of Jesus Christ. My goal, therefore, is to make the reader aware of known biblical truths through a careful hermeneutical analysis of Scripture. This book can be used as a reference when questions arise about salvation through grace in contrast to regeneration through self-effort, water baptism, and other works.

It is my sincere prayer that the reader will learn the dangers of placing the grace of God under the burden of works, observances, regulations, or moral conduct and behaviors.

I will address the errors of the *"Apostolic/Jesus Only"* doctrine that, in my opinion, have received a free ride in religious America for the last 50 years.

Many books have been written about the doctrinal errors of the Jehovah's Witnesses, the Seventh-Day Adventists, and other works-based denominations. Conversely, very few books have been written on the dangers of salvation through water baptism. With this in mind, I have been inspired to undertake the very important task of offering a biblically sound rebuttal against popular works-based denominational beliefs.

The *Apostolic/Jesus Only Doctrine*, hereafter referred to as the *Oneness Doctrine*, states that if an individual is not baptized and baptized in Jesus' name, he is not saved. Some doctrines even espouse that one must not only be baptized in water and in Jesus' name, but one also must speak in tongues in order to be filled with the Holy Ghost. These approaches to biblical doctrine are critically flawed and can lead to grave consequences.

My prayer is that this book will bring souls to repentance and to the living Christ. While some may be offended by the contents written herein, many will allow God's Spirit to speak to their hearts, see the errors of their ways, and turn to a loving and merciful God who is ready to abundantly forgive and pardon.

Hundreds of thousands of people have been hoodwinked and deceived by this simply erroneous and damnable doctrine. This book is a warning to the latter day church that what Jesus accomplished at Cavalry cannot and will not be minimized or compromised by good works, good behaviors, or by observing laws and regulations. As the clock of this age ticks to a close and the hands of time advance, there is great urgency to communicate this divine revelation: The only salvation is through Christ Jesus!

The end will not sneak up on us. The Bible tells us clearly that there will be signs, cues, alarms, and warnings to signal that the last days are upon us. Some of these signs are earthquakes, tidal waves, roaring seas, floods, fires, tsunamis, starvation, wars, unparalleled pestilences, global diseases, increased violence, terrorism and a myriad of dreadful and fearful sights. Today we live in those last days.

This book will be strength to some, a turning point to others, and a lifeline for those being changed from **religious** to **transformed** (Romans 12:2). I hope to bring light to every reader and to motivate each individual to move from a knowledge of God to a relationship with God. In the final analysis, a true relationship with God is the only thing that matters.

PART I
WATER BAPTISM

CHAPTER ONE

What Do Oneness Churches

Really Believe About God?

For years, Oneness churches were extremely vocal about their particular doctrine. This generally resulted in their congregations being small and exclusive. Their theology denies the Trinity and teaches that God revealed himself as Father in the Old Testament, as the Son in the New Testament during Christ's ministry on earth, and now as the Holy Spirit after Christ's ascension.

This doctrine unequivocally maintains that if you are not baptized in water, you cannot be saved and enter into the kingdom of heaven. Further, they teach that baptism must be by immersion and must be administered with the formula "In Jesus' name" rather than the formula *"In the Name of the Father, the Son, and the Holy Spirit"* as expressly mentioned in Matthew 28:19.

Some denominations also teach that speaking in tongues is a necessary component of salvation. They believe that only those who have spoken in tongues are really saved.

There is an emphasis that Oneness church members speak in tongues to "demonstrate" that they are saved and have the truth. Years ago, Oneness church members attempted to represent themselves in a modest and holy manner. This is to be commended. Women were not permitted to wear pants or makeup and were instructed to cover their heads. Likewise, men were to be well dressed, preferably wearing ties. The Oneness doctrine also implied that those who went to the movies or owned televisions were not "really" Christians.

Such practices are not inherently wrong and are, in many instances, good examples of propriety. However, it becomes problematic when physical presentation or unbiblical restrictions are used as a means by which a person's spirituality is judged.

However, in an attempt to attract greater numbers, Oneness churches have quietly become more liberal in their appeal.

The core beliefs haven't changed, but the churches have softened the message so drastically that a majority of the members are not even remotely aware of the doctrinal errors they espouse. They now blend in with other popular traditional Protestant denominations. Many of these congregations have become mega-churches and attract high-profile members. Some of these pastors are viewed as national spiritual leaders and are given "star" status in the religious arena.

The term "Jesus Only" is now rare and is almost never used in contemporary religious circles. In Christian educational settings those who hold this doctrinal belief are known as "Oneness Pentecostals." Yet their fundamental beliefs have not changed. Oneness Pentecostal people are numerous, but usually are divided into two main groups generally referred to as: Apostolics or Jesus only.

There are also a number of other churches and groups who don't realize grace alone is sufficient, and hold to a mixture of works, law, self-effort, and grace.

A host of non-denominational and inde-pendent Oneness churches scattered around the world have bought into this doctrine. These precious people have been teaching this doc-trine of error for many years. They have shout-ed and danced and praised God, but the scrip-ture warns about having a form of godliness, but denying the power thereof (2 Timothy 3:5). The only way to heaven is God's way and His way is through the blood of our Lord and Sav-ior, Jesus Christ (Revelation 5:9 & 7:14).

Oneness Pentecostal groups generally hold some form of the following erroneous points of doctrine:

1. Baptism is necessary and required for salvation.
2. Water baptism is what washes away sin.
3. Water baptism signs and seals a per-son's regeneration in Christ.
4. Justification by faith alone does not bring salvation.
5. There is no Trinity.
6. Jesus is God the Father.

7. Jesus and the Holy Spirit are one and the same.

8. The name of God is "Jesus."

9. There was no pre-existence of the Word as the Son. The Son existed as the Father.

10. Being born again means repentance, baptism, and speaking in tongues.

11. Water baptism and the gift of the Holy Ghost are simultaneous and indivisible.

12. Baptism must be administered with the phrase, "In the name of Jesus" instead of the phrase, *"In the name of the Father, the Son, and the Holy Spirit"* (Matthew 28:19).

13. Speaking in tongues is a necessary requirement to demonstrate that a person is saved and filled with the Holy Spirit.

14. Only Oneness people will go to heaven.

15. Water baptism is only valid when administered by an ordained Oneness minister.

The aforementioned points, each outside of the basic tenets of Christianity, can be placed into three major categories:

I. WATER BAPTISM

II. THE TRINITY

III. SALVATION BY WORKS

Each doctrinal error, as it relates to the above categories, will be addressed in detail in the following chapters.

In Part One, issues related to baptism will be addressed; in Part Two, I will discuss the Trinity; in Part Three, I will address salvation by works, behaviors and good deeds.

CHAPTER TWO

Identifying With the Family of

Christ

Water baptism is one of several observances that Christ ordained during his last days on this earth. In the great commission of Matthew 28:19-20, Jesus addresses water baptism. The Lord said, *"Go ye therefore, and teach all nations, baptizing them in the name of the Father, and of the Son, and of the Holy Ghost: 20) Teaching them to observe all things whatsoever I have commanded you: and, lo, I am with you always, even unto the end of the world. Amen."* Water baptism is integral to the body of Christ, yet it has no redemptive significance.

Water baptism is symbolic and is simply a public attestation or showing of our inclusion in God's family. It is a work of righteousness that should be observed; however, some denominational doctrines make it efficacious, meaning that it is one of the things that provide salvation. They believe that water baptism is required if one is to enter into God's grace.

This position is never stated or even implied in the Word of God. This line of thinking distracts the emphasis away from the precious blood of Jesus and Calvary's cross. There is only one scriptural condition for observing baptism. The stipulation is that one must be saved **before** observing the baptismal rite (Acts 8:36-38).

As it relates to salvation, water baptism accomplishes nothing for the one being baptized. To those watching the ceremony, the baptism signifies that person being baptized has accepted Christ and is now unashamedly a part of God's family. Water baptism symbolizes publicly that a spiritual transformation has taken place in the heart of the individual being baptized. Further, baptism in the name of Jesus, or the Father, Son, and Holy Ghost, does not make one a member of God's family. It is a wonderful celebration of our inclusion into the household of faith (Ephesians 2:18-19). Water baptism is simply a public identification with Christ and the people of God. In the future, particularly as radical Islamic groups expand with religious agendas, public conversion and baptism will take on greater significance here in America.

We are baptized publicly as an expression of faith in God. It is an initial testimony symbolizing the fact that we have died to sin and have been buried and are raised again with newness of life. Baptism is unnecessary as it relates to salvation and there is no penalty in the Word of God for not being baptized (Mark 16:16). However, it should be observed as an act of obedience. Again, water baptism is a good work and does not and cannot produce salvation and it should never be included as part of the chemistry or recipe whereby a man can obtain a transformed life.

The observances of laws, rules, and works, was the method of obtaining righteousness in Old Testament times, yet Jesus paid for all our sins on the cross of Calvary. All of the old laws, observances, and regulations to obtain righteousness were done away with. *"So now we can rejoice in our wonderful new relationship with God because our Lord Jesus Christ has made us friends of God."* Romans 5:11 (NLT).

Once an individual has accepted Christ as their personal Savior, by all means, a celebration of new life, through water baptism, is in order. Conversely, if one has already been baptized in water, and believes that the act of submersion made the individual a part of the family of Christ, he is mistaken. Repentance is necessary in order to accept Christ as one's personal Lord and Savior and should be done as quickly as possible (Revelation 2:5). The Bible says in Matthew 7:22-23, *"Many will say to me in that day, Lord, Lord, have we not prophesied in thy name? And in thy name have cast out devils? And in thy name done many wonderful works? 23) And then will I profess unto them, I never knew you: depart from me, ye that work iniquity."* This verse refers to the multitudes of good, religious, church-going people who will come before God to enter into the kingdom of heaven and be rejected outright. This is referring to religious folk.

They will have made great changes in society, improved the quality of life for many people, and even assisted some into the kingdom of heaven. However, they themselves will miss the mark because they elevated some work, such as water baptism or church attendance, over the humble way of simply accepting Christ as personal Savior (John 3:16). How awful to perform good works, to cast out demons in the name of Christ, to heal the sick, leave a wonderful legacy for mankind, and still end up lost! This should not be when we can accept Christ and what Christ alone has done. We not only point others to heaven, but we ourselves enter into God's joyful eternity only through the blood of Jesus Christ.

The Apostle Paul addressed this with the Corinthian church – a very carnal and worldly church. At one point, this church was divided as to their allegiance. Apostle Paul addressed this in I Corinthians 1:12-13. He says, 12) *"Now this I say, that every one of you saith, I am of Paul; and I of Apollos; and I of Cephas; and I of Christ. 13) Is Christ divided? Was Paul crucified for you? Or were ye baptized in the name of Paul?"* Carnality is clearly seen in this passage. There were cliques and special groups in the church at Corinth. One group aligns itself with Paul. Another wants to be associated with the black public speaker Apollos because of his great oratorical skills. Others said they were of Christ. Consequently, the Apostle Paul is forced to address this issue by asking if they were baptized in the name of Paul. Whenever you see the term "in the name of" it simply means "by the authority of."

In Verse 14 he continues, *"I thank God that I baptized none of you, but Crispus and Gaius."* Notice how Paul put baptism in its proper place. Now if baptism were indeed the instrument by which we are introduced or placed into the body of Christ or family of God, then the Apostle Paul would never have spoken of it in these terms. Many churches highlight baptism as the climax of a transformed life.

They gleefully baptize members in water because they think that it is the way to salvation, but the Apostle Paul contradicts this position. He contradicts this entire erroneous doctrine currently being espoused throughout America today. Paul does not denounce water baptism. He simply places water baptism in its proper position. He teaches emphatically that baptism does not save us. One must remember that there are no penalties in the Bible for not being baptized, but there are penalties for sin and unbelief (Mark 16:16).

I Corinthians 1:17 says, *"For Christ sent me not to baptize, but to preach the gospel: not with wisdom of words, lest the cross of Christ should be made of none effect."* As a pastor, the thrust of my ministry is not water baptism. Baptism is a peripheral activity. It is really a non-essential activity in relation to salvation. The cross of Christ is the Gospel. Baptism is not part of the Gospel. It is not part of that which saves; it has no redemptive powers. Baptism is a witness. It testifies that the individual who is being baptized has already gained salvation and is indicating publicly what has happened to him. The individual is showing that he has died to sin, was buried to sin, and has risen in Christ (Romans 6:4). He has experienced a spiritual renewal that is mirrored or figured in the baptismal experience.

Points to Ponder

1. *Water baptism is a public ceremony showing our inclusion into God's family.*

2. *As it relates to salvation, water baptism accomplishes nothing for the one being baptized.*

3. *There are no penalties in the Bible for not being baptized. There are penalties for not believing and committing sin.*

CHAPTER THREE

Understanding Water Baptism:

The Biblical Formula for Water

Baptism

Water Baptisms Place in the

Gospel

What does it mean to be "Born

of Water?"

We should all be baptized and as a minister, I do baptize. I baptize according to the words of the command of the Lord Jesus in St. Matthew 28:19, *"...baptizing them in the name of the Father, and of the Son, and of the Holy Ghost."* This verse gives us the biblical formula and process for water baptism. As recorded, the author indicates by whose authority they performed the rite of baptism. They baptized by the authority of the Father, Son, and Holy Ghost. That is why in Acts, which is a record of the baptismal experience, they were baptized in the name of or by the authority of the Lord Jesus (Acts 19:5), also in the name of the Lord (Acts 10:48). It's a recording of an onlooker stating by whose authority or edict they performed the rite of baptism.

There is only one place where Jesus commands and instructs how baptism should be performed in St. Matthew 28:19-20. He taught them to baptize in the name of the Father, and of the Son, and of the Holy Ghost.

Those are the words of the Lord Jesus to

those who are to perform the symbolic rite of baptism.

Water Baptisms Place in the Gospel

Let's examine whether water baptism has a place in the Gospel. It's very important that we examine scripture intellectually and clinically. Let's look again at I Corinthians 1:12-14. *"Now this I say, that every one of you saith, I am of Paul; and I of Apollos; and I of Cephas; and I of Christ. 13) Is Christ divided? Was Paul crucified for you? Or were ye baptized in the name of Paul? 14) I thank God that I baptized none of you, but Crispus and Gaius."* Here the Apostle Paul challenges the Corinthian Church because of an inordinate emphasis on baptism and on the individuals who administered the baptism. Paul is not minimizing baptism; he is simply putting it in its proper place.

Let us be clear. The scripture does not show or suggest that any of the apostles were baptized in Christian baptism or in the name of the Father, Son, and Holy Ghost and certainly not in "Jesus' Name". None! Not one! Yet they were all filled with the Holy Ghost when they were in the upper room together. This is specifically recorded for us; none of them were even baptized in water. The Lord Jesus did teach baptism. However, he never intended for water baptism to compete with His blood. When Jesus was baptized by John the Baptist, it was not to get saved but to simply identity himself with John's message of righteousness and to fulfill all righteousness (Matthew 3:15).

As it relates to the Gospel, water baptism is relegated to a nonessential position. If water baptism was essential for salvation, there is no way God would have influenced the Apostle Paul to speak of water baptism in such casual tones. Baptism would have been spoken of in glowing, immediate, and pressing tones had it impacted our spiritual standing with God.

The Apostle Paul is telling us very distinctly that water baptism is not necessary for salvation. If you look further at I Corinthians 1:17 Paul says, *"For Christ sent me not to baptize, but to preach the Gospel."* Here he is intentionally contrasting water baptism with the Gospel. We can be sure that the Apostle Paul is not espousing his own understanding, but this is God's doing because all scripture is given by inspiration of God (II Timothy 3:16). Water baptism, like communion, tithing, church attendance, moral living, being kind and compassionate, passing out Christian literature, and feeding the poor, clothing the naked etc., should be observed with all diligence. None of these, however, have any redemptive significance! The Gospel message is simply the good news of our purchased salvation through the blood of Jesus.

Let me be clear; **water baptism cannot save!** Period. It has no miraculous, spiritual, or efficacious purpose or function and should never be included in the Gospel message.

What does it mean to be "Born of Water?"

A Lesson from Nicodemus - St. John 3:1-6

St. John 3:1-2 states, *"There was a man of*

the Pharisees, named Nicodemus, a ruler of the Jews: 2) The same came to Jesus by night, and said unto Him, Rabbi, we know that thou art a teacher come from God: for no man can do these miracles that thou doest, except God be with Him." One must observe the contextual substance of this conversation. In Verse 3, Jesus is replying to Nicodemus, *"Jesus answered and said unto him, Verily, verily, I say unto thee, except a man be born again, he cannot see the kingdom of God."* A careful reading will reveal that birth is referred to twice in this passage. Jesus used the term "born again." Being born **again** assumes that a person was born a **first time**. There is an assumption of two births here.

Following the consistency in the context, we see that Nicodemus replies to the words of the Lord. In Verse 4, *"Nicodemus saith unto Him, how can a man be born when he is old? Can he enter the second time into his mother's womb, and be born?"* Notice, birth is referred to twice in Verse 4. So we see birth twice in Verse 3 and twice in Verse 4. This text requires a closer examination in order to understand what Jesus is teaching. One must determine what the first birth is and what is the second birth? Our problem is to find out precisely what kind of birth is being discussed.

Nicodemus' mindset is on the mechanics of natural birth. He asks, "Can a man be born when he is old? Can he enter the second time into his mother's womb and be born?" Nicodemus is referring to conception, carrying the child to full term, and then the process by which the child is brought forth. This is Nicodemus' understanding of Jesus' terminology "born again."

The misinterpretation of Verse 5 results in some churches erroneously taking the doctrine of baptismal regeneration and teaching that water baptism is essential for salvation. Baptism is not even mentioned in Verse 5. *"Jesus answered, Verily, verily, I say unto thee, except a man be born of water and of the Spirit, he cannot enter into the kingdom of God."* What does "born of water" mean? Jesus is simply replying to the mindset of Nicodemus.

The answer is in Verse 6, *"That which is born of the flesh is flesh; and that which is born of the Spirit is spirit."* So Jesus defines Verse 5 for us in Verse 6. When Jesus says *"born of water"* in Verse 5, he's talking about physical birth, and then the new birth. This is the meaning of born again. Born again is by the spirit. There are only two kinds of births mentioned in Verse 6, a natural birth and spiritual birth. Jesus says nothing about a water baptismal birth.

What then is "born of water"? Every human being that ever lived was born of water. That's the most common experience of all human beings, white, yellow, red, or black. Jesus was dealing practically with a man who was asking very basic questions. When a woman's water sack bursts, where the baby lived for nine months, that mother knows that the baby is coming. This is what Jesus meant when he said, "born of water." Any interpretation of baptism here actually violates the text. In this dialogue, the only references to birth involve physical birth and spiritual birth.

The crux of this verse separates the natural from the spiritual. It contrasts the heavenly with the worldly and clarifies the difference between an earthly birth and spiritual transformation. This passage should never be even remotely associated with water baptism and certainly not regeneration through water baptism.

CHAPTER FOUR

Water Baptism Unveiled

The Danger of Regeneration

through Water Baptism

Pride is the foundation of any attempt to substitute good works or other rituals for what God has done! God has ordained the means to our salvation, which in scripture includes not just our regeneration, but also our sanctification and, one day, our final deliverance from sin as we come into the presence of the risen Christ (Romans 8:23-25; I John 3:1-3). A truly regenerated person will live a godly life and heed the truths of God's Word. By these means, he gives evidence of the work of the Spirit in his heart, making his *"calling and election sure"* (II Peter 1:10).

Man has always attempted to circumvent God's commandments and the grace that God has provided for our salvation. The unmerited favor God has provided is too basic for the learned and erudite, too simple for the astute, too foolish for the wise, and too accessible for the deep and ponderous. *"But God hath chosen the foolish things of the world to confound the wise; and God hath chosen the weak things of the world to confound the things which are mighty; And base things of the world, and things which are despised, hath God chosen, yea, and things which are not, to bring to nought things that are: That no flesh should glory in his presence."* (I Corinthians 1:27-29).

Instead of accepting what God has already done, man attempts to bring God's ways into the realm of human experience. Saved by "grace through faith" excludes man's involvement and includes no place for earthly intervention (Ephesians 2:8). Water baptism in this regard is a damnable diversion. Pride causes mankind to want to play a role in transforming lives and changing hearts. Pride causes attempts to get around the Word of God to circumvent the Word by implementing man-made guidelines. These attempts are not new.

Satan's first unsuccessful attempt to circumvent God was in heaven, and multitudes of the angels fell with him. In the Garden of Eden, man again attempted to get around God by eating of the forbidden fruit.

The serpent appealed to Adam and Eve's

pride in causing them to think they could assist God and improve on His plan. Their disobedience almost 7,000 years ago impacted not only their future, but impacted and will continue to impact all future generations. They had no idea what their decision would cost them and all of humanity.

The Danger of Regeneration through Water Baptism

This doctrine of regeneration through water baptism in the name of Jesus, while appearing harmless, is a heresy to deceive thousands of honest and sincere seekers of God. Many will seek to enter into heaven and not be able (Matthew 7:21-23).

Now most people are not seeking to enter into heaven, so this is obviously not referring to the general masses of the world's populations. To seek means to focus. The individual who seeks is totally focused on what he or she is trying to find. It is upmost in the mind, producing a one dimensional endeavor.

Most people are not seeking to enter into heaven, but Jesus said of those who are seeking, many of them would not be able, because the search is based on the wrong thing, as in the case of salvation through water baptism. This verse is referring to religious people, those who are practicing, faithful, and committed to the wrong god.

Anyone who believes that water baptism remits sin is still in his sins. Anyone who believes that joining a church or observing the Sabbath will result in the remission of his sins, will remain in sin. Unfortunately, anyone who dies in sin, will go to hell and that is not what we want.

The book of Hebrews explains it fully. Hebrews 9:1 9-22 says, *"For when Moses had spoken every precept to all the people according to the law, he took the blood of calves and of goats, with water, and scarlet wool, and hyssop, and sprinkled both the book, and all the people, 20) Saying, this is the blood of the testament which God hath enjoined unto you. 21)*

Moreover He sprinkled with blood both the tabernacle, and all the vessels of the ministry. 22) And almost all things are by the law purged with blood; and without shedding of blood is no remission." Is that clear enough? It is not water baptism; it is the blood. Remission has already been provided. Redemption has already been provided. Forgiveness of sins has already been provided. The only thing we can possibly do is to accept what has already been done.

God has provided salvation as a gift to mankind. If we are to do anything to obtain it or secure it, it is no longer a gift. If one has to acquire salvation by performing a work or a deed, it has not been gifted.

It has been earned. Romans 3:20 says, *"Therefore by the deeds of the law there shall no flesh be justified in his sight: for by the law is the knowledge of sin."* That is across the board, all encompassing. That includes circumcision, offerings, baptism, feet washing, visiting the sick, or any other good deed or moral behavior. Verse 21 continues, *"But now the righteousness of God without the law is manifested, being witnessed by the law and the prophets; 22) Even the righteousness of God which is by faith of Jesus Christ unto all and upon all them that believe; for there is no difference."* By what? Faith. Faith and works are two different things. Works accompany faith, but a man is not justified by his works.

Belief is a mental exercise. You believe in your heart and you confess with your mouth (Romans 10:9-10). That's all. Verse 23 says, *"For all have sinned, and come short of the glory of God; 24). Being justified freely by His grace through the redemption that is in Christ Jesus:"* It is free and you don't have to do anything to receive it. Verse 25 says, *"Whom God hath set forth to be a propitiation through faith in His blood, to declare His righteousness for the remission of sins that are past, through the forbearance of God."* Salvation was provided and secured at Calvary. You were not there, but Jesus was there. He said on the cross, *"It is finished."* All we have to do is accept what He has freely given.

When I complete my sermons I don't ask if there is anyone in the audience who is ready to be baptized. No, I ask if there is anyone who is ready to receive Jesus. Baptism is subsequent to salvation and not necessary for salvation. Faith in His blood gains remission. What is it that justifies mankind? Belief. Verse 26 says, *"To declare, I say, at this time His righteousness: That He might be just, and the justifier of Him which believeth in Jesus."*

This verse eliminates any possibility that justification is accomplished through baptism or being filled with the Holy Ghost and speaking in tongues. This scripture says that He justifies him that believes in Jesus.

Anyone who depends on water baptism or the filling of the Holy Ghost for salvation is not saved. Any church that teaches salvation by water baptism is in grave error, regardless of the size of the membership or the charisma of the leader. Salvation is rooted in the blood of Jesus Christ. Some churches, even in these end times, do not speak very often about the blood. They don't emphasize the blood. Romans 3:31 continues, *"Do we then make void the law through faith? God forbid: Yea, we establish the law."* It is all based on faith in the blood of Jesus.

Romans 4:1-2 says, *"What shall we say then that Abraham our father, as pertaining to the flesh, hath found? 2) For if Abraham were justified by works, he hath whereof to glory; but not before God."* This text refers to every kind of works and all works. Abraham was making animal sacrifices of all kind. Even under the law, the people were only justified by faith and these acts and deeds were simply an expression of their faith. Verse 3 says, *"For what saith the scripture? Abraham believed God, and it was counted unto him for righteousness."* This is the same thing we do today. We believe God and receive salvation.

Let's go further. Romans 4:4 says, *"Now to Him that worketh is the reward not reckoned of grace, but of debt."* If baptism was required for salvation, then God owes salvation to any individual who was baptized. Salvation, in this theory, would have been earned. Again, if it is earned through baptism, it is not grace. However, God owes us nothing! God is not indebted to us, we are indebted to God. Sin left us deserving judgment and hell. Nevertheless, God saves us by His grace, through faith in the blood of the Lord Jesus.

The devil thought he had us but Jesus stood in the gap for us. He took our place and because of Jesus we can all be free from the guilt and stain of sin. It's all about Jesus and what he has done for mankind.

If water baptism has the power to regenerate the heart and mind of man and is to be the determinate factor in where we spend eternity, then serious technical questions surrounding its implementation must be asked. Is full immersion in water the method of regeneration? Will partial immersion suffice? Is baptism by sprinkling tolerable? Does the kind of water (tap, lake, spring water, etc.) assist or deter in any way? If, in fact, water can transform souls, can it also heal bodies of diverse diseases and ailments such as cancer and HIV? What would happen to a person who has the desire and faith to be saved but is stuck in a desert or someplace where water is unavailable as happened with the thieves on the cross? (Luke 23:39-43).

These are some of the questions that must be addressed if one truly believes in regeneration by water. When you understand that baptism has no meaning as it relates to salvation, then all of the controversy over in whose name one must be baptized becomes neutralized. Salvation is through grace alone. The blood of Jesus, shed at Calvary's cross, is the only way to eternal life with Christ. If a person has accepted Christ by faith as their personal Savior, he has been transformed and is now a candidate for water baptism. However, if a person is not saved and under the impression that water baptism will save and transform him, then that person is basing his destiny on a work and is thereby jeopardizing his eternal destiny.

PART II:

THE TRINITY

CHAPTER FIVE

Understanding the Trinity

Oneness Doctrine

Pseudo-Trinity Doctrine

Examples of the Trinity

Something happened in 1914 at a Pentecostal World Convention in Los Angeles, California. There were hundreds of people who came to commemorate the outpouring of the Holy Ghost in 1906. It was the great Azusa Street outpouring that was spearheaded by a one-eyed itinerant, illiterate, African-American preacher. He was a super intelligent man, but illiterate in the sense of not having a formal education. His name was William J. Seymour. This was a man of prayer, one of God's choice servants, who was used to bring Pentecost to America, yet God knows how to use people who are despised, weak, and discounted, to accomplish his will. Every Pentecostal organization in the world, of which I am aware, had its beginning with William Seymour and the Azusa Street outpouring in California.

Belief in Trinity Challenged

God poured out his Spirit mightily at Azusa Street, but during a subsequent convention, the enemy came in. A man stood up and said he had discovered that the name of the God-head was Jesus. Because many people did not truly understand the Trinity, many ceased to believe in the Trinity as being the Father, the Son, and the Holy Spirit. This man's false doc-trine stated that the Godhead was really one person who eternally manifests himself as three persons. At one point, He's the Father, at another point, He's the Son, and still at anoth-er point He's the Holy Ghost. This doctrine to-tally negates the Trinity. He based his theory on Acts 2:38, Acts 19:5, and Acts 10:48. In each of these texts, there is a variation of the name of the Lord Jesus. According to his "reve-lation", he discovered that the name of the Fa-ther, Son, and Holy Ghost is really **Jesus**.

Simply stated, he believed that the name of the Father was Jesus, the name of the Son was Jesus, and the name of the Holy Ghost was Jesus, and this one person displays himself in various roles.

That is simply not the case. That was a ter-rible and satanic error. The name of the Father is not Jesus, and the name of the Holy Ghost is not Jesus. This doctrine believes that "Son" is not a name and "Father" is not a name. This is erroneous.

There is a difference between a common and a proper noun. A proper noun represents the name of a specific person, place, or thing. A common noun is a noun referring to a person, place, or thing in a general sense. When you look in a dictionary, you see the son and father are common nouns. The scripture lets us know they are also proper nouns and names. In Isaiah 9:6 we read, *"For unto us a child is born, unto us a Son is given: and the government shall be upon His shoulder: and His name shall be called, Wonderful, Counsellor, the Mighty God, the Everlasting Father, the Prince of Peace."* Some people say Father is not a name. This is simply a scholastic and scriptural error.

The Father is the name of the first person in the Trinity. He is Father. That's His name. The Son is the name of the second person in the Trinity and the Holy Ghost is the third person in the Trinity. <u>All three are distinctive persons, yet they are one.</u> By definition, a trinity is a group having three distinct members, parts, or facets.

The Father gave the Son. The Son gave his life and returned back to the Father and sent the Holy Ghost. He referred to the Holy Ghost using the personal pronoun "He". Jesus said in St. John 16:13, *"Howbeit, when He, the Spirit of truth, is come, He will guide you into all truth: for He shall not speak of Himself, but whatsoever He shall hear, that shall He speak: and He will shew you things to come."*

Over and over again we are told of the personhood of the Holy Ghost, the personhood of Christ, and the personhood of the Father. They are three distinct persons, yet one God.

Jesus makes the clearest distinction between himself and the Holy Ghost by stating in I John 16:7, *"It is expedient for you that I go away: for if I go not away, the Comforter <u>will not</u> come unto you; but if I <u>depart</u>, I will <u>send</u>*

<u>*him*</u> *unto you."*

Oneness Doctrine

Another doctrinal position taught is the Oneness theory. This theory claims that God, Jesus, and the Holy Ghost are one spirit that changes forms depending on the situation. This belief alleges that God has lived throughout endless ages in solitary confinement. There was only one person in the Godhead. This doctrinal position negates the Trinity espousing that when Jesus was on the earth, there was no God in heaven, and when the Holy Ghost came, Jesus no longer existed, and when Jesus was on the earth, the throne was empty. However, to the contrary, when Jesus was on the earth He told his disciples to pray unto the Father who was in heaven. I make reference to the world's most well-known prayer, commonly called the Lord's Prayer. Jesus while on earth seen and touched by man, taught us to pray to the Father *"which art in heaven"* (Matthew 6:9). He's telling us to pray to the Father, the first person of the Trinity, who is not on earth like he is, but in heaven. He prayed unto the Father who was in another location, heaven. One time he prayed to his Father until great drops of sweat like blood came off his brow (Luke 22:42-44). Now either his Father was in heaven, or Jesus was misguided. Jesus was never misguided because the Father was in heaven. While Jesus was on earth he referred to the Father in heaven over 18 times.

Pseudo-Trinity Doctrine

Then there is a position that espouses a pseudo-trinity, a belief that the Trinity is actually a manifestation. This belief states that God can manifest himself as Jesus, who can manifest himself as the Holy Ghost, and the Holy Ghost can manifest himself as the Father. This "manifestation" view also negates the Trinity and in essence the power of the true and living God and is another misinterpretation of the scriptures.

We must understand that God eternally exists as three distinct persons. Once it is understood that there is an absolute Trinity in the Godhead; that the Father is not the Son, the Son is not the Holy Ghost, and the Holy Ghost is not the Father, then this confusion regarding the accurate name falls into its proper perspective. The Godhead consists of the Father, the Son, and the Holy Spirit, and these three are one. I am not espousing polytheism or many gods, there is only one God, eternally existing in 3 distinct persons, the Father, the Son, and the Holy Ghost.

Examples of the Trinity in the Universe

Psalms 19:1 says that *"The heavens declare the glory of God; and the firmament sheweth his handiwork."* God so incredibly revealed himself in his wonderful creation of the universe. He so beautifully declared the nature of the triune God in his formation of all that we see, hear, feel, taste, and smell. Our universe consists of three elements: time, space, and matter. While these three elements are distinctly different they are tied together as one to make up our universe. Time is not space, space is not matter, and matter is neither time nor space. Yet, together they are one in the makeup of the universe. If you take any element away you no longer have the universe, as we know it. Time is not manifested as space, and space does not manifest itself as matter. If you take away time what do you have? Nothing, because time is used to determine the age of matter. If you take away space there is nothing to hold matter. All three are unique, have distinct qualities, and like the Trinity, all three exist as one.

Trinity Seen At Jesus Baptism

In St. Luke 3:22 as Jesus was baptized, the Bible says *"And the Holy Ghost descended in a bodily shape like a dove upon him, and a voice came from heaven, which said, Thou art my beloved Son; in thee I am well pleased."* Here our Lord Jesus, the second person of the Trinity is being baptized, and something happens for the benefit of future generations to come. The Holy

Spirit, the third person of the Trinity, descends from the skies in a bodily shape so that we know he is distinctively different. To crystallize this, the Father, the first person of the Trinity completes the triune makeup of God and makes a clear distinction by pointing to his son and declaring: *"This is my beloved son in whom I am well pleased"*. Here we have a clear and concise scenario of the Trinity in action.

The Trinity: In Creation

In the Old Testament, we see an example of the Trinity. God introduces the plurality of his nature in Genesis 1:26. *"And God said, Let us make man in our image, after our likeness . . ."* The personal pronoun just jumps out at us. You see the plurality that's stated in the God-head. It's not suggested, it's stated right in the first book of the Bible. Who was God talking to? He was talking to the Son and the Holy Ghost who we have found to be a part of the triune God. God Introduced himself to mankind as the creator of the earth. His introduction included the plurality of the Godhead.

God Created in man a triune component of spirit (I Corinthians 2:11), soul (Mark 12:30), and body (I Corinthians 6:19-20). The spirit in man is the God conscious, the soul is the self conscious, and the body is the world conscious. The spirit is what relates to God and both spirit and mind live in the body.

In the New Testament in Matthew 28:19 the Lord Jesus speaks of the Trinity in very clear terms. Jesus says, *"Go ye therefore, and teach all nations, baptizing them in the name of the Father, and of the Son, and of the Holy Ghost."* That's by the authority of the Trinity. While I am not claiming that this formula of baptism in the name of the Father, Son, and Holy Ghost has any efficacious value, it does show the clarity of the Trinity. Baptism in the name of the Father, Son, and Holy Ghost, baptism in Jesus' name, or a combination of them both will not save your soul. Only the blood of Jesus has divine transformational power.

The Trinity: Distinct Wills, Emotions, Intellects

The Trinity eternally exists as three persons with three different sets of intellects, wills, and emotions. The Lord Jesus said to His Father when He was praying in the Garden of Gethsemane, (St. Matthew 26:39) *"Not as I will, but as thou wilt."* He is saying that there is a will that the Father has that is specifically the Father's will. There is a will that is specifically the Son's will. However, because these three eternally exist in complete unity in the Godhead, Jesus submits to his Father. While taking on the sins of mankind, our sins caused a temporary separation in the relationship between the Father and the Son, a separation that had never before existed, and Jesus submits to the will of the Father. Jesus had to take on the incomprehensible enormity of sins of mankind past, present, and future sins that mankind has committed and sins that mankind will commit. This caused our ever undefiled Christ, who knew no sin, to respond and for the first time in recorded scripture, to reveal the different will and intellects of the Godhead. For our sakes, Jesus submitted his will to that of his Father. Jesus paid the ultimate price for our salvation with his blood. Praise God we can stand justified by the blood of Jesus.

The Trinity Illuminated

In the Book of Revelation, we see the Son taking the scroll out of the right hand of the Father (Revelation 5:6-7). In Hebrews 10:12 He is seated on the right hand of the Father. These instances show the distinction in the Godhead. St. Matthew 24:36 shows the three distinct persons of the trinity when Jesus tells us that only God knows the day and hour when the Son of man will return. The book of Isaiah contains a glaring scripture that not only depicts the intelligent, probing, and inquisitive mind of God, but the plurality and distinction that is in the Godhead. Isaiah 48:16 says, *"Come ye near unto me, hear ye this; I have not spoken in secret from the beginning; from the time that it was, there am I: and*

now the Lord God, and His Spirit, hath sent me."
Our Lord and Savior Jesus Christ was talking.
He's the one that was sent by the Lord God, who
is the Father, and the Holy Spirit. Here you see
the Trinity. The Trinity consists of the Father,
The Son, and Holy Spirit and these three distinct
persons are one.

Acknowledging Truth

A while ago, I had lunch with an apostolic
minister. I began to clinically examine his position and he examined mine. He is a leading
apostolic minister and by the time we finished,
he had become a Trinitarian. He didn't change
churches and he didn't change his doctrinal
position immediately because he has been a
leading apostolic minister for years. He is an
intelligent, rational man and a fine minister.
Because our conversation was not conducted
in front of either of our congregations, neither
one of us had to posture for people. He didn't
have to protect his flank and I didn't have to
protect my position. I didn't have to try to look

great, smart, and wonderful, and neither did he. We were simply able to examine scripture in a non-threatening, non-argumentative fashion. He felt respected and valued by me and I felt respected and valued by him. We clinically examined the scriptures verse by verse and line by line, word by word, and precept by precept. We both knew that arguing and fighting over the Word of God (especially in public) accomplishes nothing but division, separation, and confusion and the Word says "God is not the author of confusion". Yet I understood the seriousness of this issue that if in fact he was right and water baptism is what saves a person, then I was on my way to an eternal hell (along with my parishioners) for a lack of faith and not believing in what truly saves and transforms a person (II Corinthians 5:17). He also understood that if he were wrong, he and his parishioners would end up in eternal hell. Neither one of us wanted to go to hell or allow the other person to go to hell.

He finally said, "Pastor Arrington, I don't

know many ministers like you. You Trinitarians believe in three gods." I said, "No, you're mistaken there. Trinitarians don't believe in three gods or polytheism. <u>The Bible describes one God eternally existing in three distinct persons</u>." This minister acknowledged after examining the scriptures that the Trinity does exists and only Jesus' blood can wash us from sin. What he did in his church is something I'm not sure about, but I can only pray that he came to true faith in what Jesus accomplished at the Cross of Calvary and that we are saved by grace and grace alone!

PART III:

WORKS OF

RIGHTEOUSNESS

CHAPTER SIX

Salvation through Works

The Apostle Paul had problems with people in his ministry who would espouse anything but grace, especially the Pharisees. The Pharisees were not fully dependent on the blood of Jesus. If an individual depends on anything but the blood of the Lord Jesus for salvation, he is depending upon the wrong thing. Nothing can save us or wash away our sins but the blood of Jesus. Taking this erroneous doctrinal position of salvation partially dependent on what Jesus has done and partially dependent on what you have done will not save you. It's all Jesus or nothing. The hymn says, "Jesus paid it all, and all to him I owe. Sin had left a crimson stain, He washed it white as snow."

If water baptism was necessary for salvation, then Jesus didn't have to suffer, bleed, die, and his resurrection would be meaningless. If God had to accept us because of our work, or keeping the law, God would be indebted to us and he would owe us. But that is absolutely not the case!

Mankind is notorious for finding ways to

work out their own soul salvation. A work is something that you do, something that *you* accomplish or perform. It can be an act such as one of obedience or a deed. It can be labor or simply an effort, but it is almost always something that is done physically. Man, by nature, has an inclination to depend on works.

Jesus has provided a way whereby no works are needed or accepted for salvation. It is a free gift. It is given because God is compassionate and full of grace, which is God's unmerited and undeserved favor. Grace provides favor that is not merited. Grace is absolutely freely given. If one must complete the act of baptism in order to complete the act of salvation, as some churches believe, or one must pass out literature, as some kingdom halls believe, grace is not a part of the process.

If baptism is necessary for salvation, then the word grace can be taken out of the scripture. That would mean this beautiful word "grace," which is a New Testament term, has no application at all. We are saved by grace.

Period. It's called a free gift over and over again, almost as if God was being redundant. Now if it's a gift, you know it's free. God wants us to understand that we can't do anything to earn this particular "so-great salvation." It has nothing to do with works. Eleven times in scripture salvation is referred to as a gift.

In fact, this is the reason why the Apostle Paul said, *"God sent me not to baptize."* (I Corinthians 1:17). He put water baptism in a distinct nonessential category. In Acts 15:1 Paul says, *"And certain men which came down from Judaea taught the brethren, and said, except ye be circumcised after the manner of Moses, ye cannot be saved."* The Pharisees emphasized circumcision. Circumcision is a work just like baptism.

Now, this is the Old Testament and early part of the New Testament counterpart of the modern day doctrinal statement that says unless you're baptized in Jesus' name you cannot be saved. Both consist of a work that the individual must perform.

The Apostle Paul had trouble with the Judaizers who insisted upon introducing circumcision into the recipe for salvation, something God never did. The frustration Paul experienced dealing with the Judaizers is evident in Galatians chapter 5. Verse 1 states, *"Stand fast therefore in the liberty wherewith Christ hath made us free, and be not entangled again with the yoke of bondage."* Paul is saying, "don't go back into works because they never save; they are only an expression of your willingness to obey. You identify yourself with the God of Abraham, Isaac, and Jacob through the keeping of these works; but works *never* save. Verse 2 continues, *"Behold, I Paul say unto you, that if ye be circumcised, Christ shall profit you nothing."* Remember circumcision is the counterpart of modern day "regeneration or salvation through water baptism." It insists upon baptism as that capstone experience that ushers a person into salvation.

In Galatians 5:3 Paul says, *"For I testify again to every man that is circumcised, that he is a debtor to do the whole law. 4) Christ is be-come of no effect unto you, whosoever of you are justified by the law; ye are fallen from grace."* Remember, if it's grace, it means un-merited favor. That means you didn't and couldn't do anything to get it. If you had to do something to get it, then it's not grace. If you had to be baptized to get it, it's not grace. It's not free. It's not a gift. As it relates to salvation, water baptism profits the one who is being baptized absolutely nothing. Verse 5 says, *"For we through the Spirit wait for the hope of right-eousness by faith."*

Faith and works as they relate to salvation, do not cohabitate. They are on two different spheres and are worlds apart. According to Ga-latians 3:11, *"The just shall live by faith."* Faith will eventually produce good works, but good works come **after** a transformed life through the blood of Jesus.

The Judaizers said, "Let's live by works." Those who are given to works today say, "Let's live by water baptism." The doctrine does have some belief in the blood; but it also teaches that in order to complete the transaction of salvation, you must be baptized and that the ceremony must be performed using the words "in Jesus' name." What a tragedy. In this mistaken doctrine, faith, grace, nor mercy are involved.

The term "mercy" refers to escaping a deserved judgment. Grace is receiving favor that we did not merit or earn. So the scripture says in Galatians 5:6, *"For in Jesus Christ neither circumcision availeth anything, nor uncircumcision; but faith which worketh by love."* That's it, beloved. It's faith and grace. It's faith in the blood of the Lord Jesus. It's so very important that we get this.

Mixing Grace

AND

Water Baptism

Galatians 6:12 says, *"As many as desire to make a fair shew in the flesh, they constrain you to be circumcised;"* Now there are people today who constrain you to be baptized in Jesus' name as if baptism were one of the meritorious or efficacious things that complete the transaction of salvation. The only thing that completes the transaction of salvation is what Christ did for you and me on the cross. He was offered once for sins. Once. There is no more sacrifice for sins than Christ and what he has already accomplished for us.

Continuing with Verse 12, *"only lest they should suffer persecution for the cross of Christ. 13) For neither they themselves who are circumcised keep the law; but desire to have you circumcised, that they may glory in your flesh."* It is the flesh that is baptized in water, and it is the flesh that is circumcised. Some, when baptized in water testify, "I'm saved, sanctified, and baptized in Jesus' name" as though baptism has something to do with their salvation. If anyone bases their salvation even partly on water baptism, they simply are not saved. It would be similar to basing your salvation partly on the blood of Jesus and partly on your educational degrees, or partly on your income. That person, regardless of how religious, good, or moral, unfortunately, has no part in the kingdom of God. That is a tragedy. In Verse 14 the Apostle Paul writes, *"But God forbid that I should glory, save in the cross of our Lord Jesus Christ, by whom the world is crucified unto me, and I unto the world."* So, we're to glory not in what we do or accomplish. We are to glory in the cross, not in water baptism. We should glory in salvation gained by Christ's sacrifice for us.

Jesus taught His disciples to baptize, so baptism is something that should be done. However, it is not done to obtain salvation; it is done to express salvation. When baptism is done to obtain salvation, it becomes a work, and God in essence becomes indebted to you. It becomes a work of debt instead of grace.

It is no more a free gift. It is something that

God owes you simply because you performed an act, deed, toil, or work. This is the same thing that the circumcisers were teaching when they said unless you are circumcised you cannot be saved.

Of course this grieved the heart of the Apostle Paul because the foundation of salvation was being attacked. If this doctrine was allowed to continue it would neutralize salvation through the death and resurrection at Calvary. All the brethren at Jerusalem had a conference to determine upon what they should base their salvation. Acts 15:5-6 describes a convention, of sorts, when the apostles, elders, and church leaders came together to discuss salvation by circumcision, works, or grace. It says, *"But there rose up certain of the sect of the Pharisees which believed, saying, that it was needful to circumcise them, and to command them to keep the law...And the apostles and elders came together for to consider of this matter."*

Jesus had already fulfilled all the laws of Moses. For example, when the Israelites came out of Egypt they sacrificed lambs, oxen, doves and bullocks, shedding the blood and sprinkling it on the doorposts. The Lord Jesus Christ made these acts unnecessary. The Lord said, "*When I see the blood, I will pass over you.*" (Exodus 12:23). That was the guarantee of their safety. The blood of the Lamb, was a type of the blood of Christ, the Lamb of God, who was going to shed His blood for the salvation of all mankind to obtain their salvation.

At this gathering of church leaders, it was decided that circumcision was an unnecessary work that actually put a yoke on Christians causing them to err from the grace of God. Peter told this group in Acts 15:11 "*But we believe that through the grace of the Lord Jesus Christ we shall be saved, even as they.*" The Spirit of God is telling the church today the same thing He told the church in biblical times.

It is by grace alone that we are saved, through the blood of Jesus. It's not through circumcision, water baptism, observing the

Sabbath, church membership, giving to the poor, living a moral life or other good and moral productive works and behaviors. It is only the blood of Jesus Christ.

CHAPTER SEVEN

The Error of Salvation by Works

Does the Holy Ghost Come to

Save?

The scripture addresses error and its tragic effects on individuals and societies. The Bible tells us in I John 4:6, *"We are of God: he that knoweth God heareth us; he that is not of God heareth not us. Hereby know we the spirit of truth, and the spirit of error."* Water baptism and the filling of the Holy Ghost are commands of the Lord. Baptism is an act of obedience. To be filled with the Holy Ghost is receiving power to be a witness. These are two distinct experiences different from salvation. Salvation was secured only at Calvary through the blood of Jesus.

There are even some Trinitarian ministers who are now captivated by fear and they are moving toward this "oneness or apostolic" error.

Some Trinitarian ministers are so fearful of the apostolic doctrine that they are even joining this erroneous doctrine. Their fear results from not wanting to omit a seemingly important component of salvation and be lost, while not realizing that Christ fulfilled every component at Calvary. Some ministers who solely believe in salvation through grace and grace alone baptize "in the name of the Father, and of the Son, and of the Holy Ghost in Jesus' name and it has nothing to do with works because they know baptism saves no one! Some Trinitarians however, baptize in the name of the Father, Son, and Holy Ghost in Jesus' name out of fear of this doctrine. Some are now only baptizing in "Jesus' Name". This method is in error and unnecessary.

They're giving a kind of acquiescence to this doctrine of inaccuracy. Those that do this are moving in the direction of error instead of explaining and illuminating the scripture and causing those who espouse this doctrine to move in the direction of truth. Since baptism has no power of regeneration, simply baptizing in error has no adverse effects unless the baptism is done to receive salvation. At that point that person is still outside of the ark of safety and is not saved.

Erroneous Teachings on the Holy Ghost

Jesus told his disciples to return to Jerusalem that they might be endued with power. In Acts 2:4 the Bible tells us how *"And they were all filled with the Holy Ghost and began to speak with other tongues."* Jesus also told us in Acts 1:8 that, *"But ye shall receive power, after that the Holy Ghost is come upon you."* He didn't say ye shall receive salvation. The Holy Ghost is not in competition with Jesus to provide salvation. The Holy Ghost has a particular function. Jesus and His death at Calvary is the only provision for salvation.

John baptized people at the Jordan River. Jesus also baptized people, but he didn't do it to save them. There are people today who will tell you if you are not baptized in water, using the words "in Jesus' name", and filled with the Holy Ghost, and speak in tongues, you're not saved. In other words, if you're baptized in Jesus' name but have not been filled with the Holy Ghost and speak in tongues, you're still not saved. If you just have baptism, you're not saved. If you just have the Holy Ghost you're not saved.

One question you can ask yourself is, "How can you be filled with the Holy Ghost and not be saved? How can you actually have the Spirit of God, the third person of the Trinity in your life and be filled and not be saved?" Bearing in mind that all believers are baptized by one spirit into the body of Christ (I Corinthians 12:13).

Being filled with the Holy Ghost is another and subsequent experience where you speak in tongues and are endued with power. That's the definition that Jesus gave of what it means to be filled with the Holy Ghost. The Holy Ghost is power that we can access as born again Christians. You are not saved by speaking in tongues, getting "happy" in church or by coming out of water feeling chills down your spine. In Acts 2:4, those in the upper room were saved and washed in the blood of Jesus who were anticipating the filling of the Holy Spirit. If more Christians would access the power of the Holy Ghost we would see more miracles, signs, and wonders in our neighborhoods, on our college campuses, we'd see the homeless housed, the sick and imprisoned getting a visit and revival breaking out in our churches all over the world, especially in America. Speaking in tongues is beneficial for the Christian but it does not save you. I Corinthians 14:6 says, *"Now, brethren, if I come unto you speaking with tongues, what shall I profit you, except I shall speak to you either by revelation, or by knowledge, or by prophesying, or by doctrine"?* Paul here exhorts the church at Corinth to use speaking in tongues wisely and not as barbarians (Verse 11) so that the church may increase and produce. Salvation was paid for at Calvary. Remember that works and behaviors can never save. Works emphasizes the individual. The individual puts on the robe, goes down in the water, he expresses his faith. It is the person performing the act. It can be called an act of faith or obedience; but whatever it is called, it is a work and works can never save you.

I'm so glad that Jesus didn't leave it to man to complicate and make salvation difficult, and that *He* did it all at Calvary. Man's ways are always inferior to God's ways. Man's methods lead to confusion. God's ways are simple, clear and plain. God made it so that everyone could receive it. Salvation is handicapped accessible. The deaf, the maimed, the dumb and even the blind can freely and easily access it. God made it so available that the imprisoned, the free, the richest and the poorest, the best of society and the worse of society can receive it. Regardless of geographic location, land, air, or water, God's salvation is accessible through the blood of Jesus. Different languages, cultures, and any other barriers are nullified by faith in Christ. Only God could create a plan of salvation so totally comprehensive and equally accessible to all.

CHAPTER EIGHT

Grace: God's Unconditional Love

The Gospel Message of Jesus

Christ

The Gospel in Operation

Throughout time, man has attempted to create methods to gain entrance to God and redeem himself. Mankind has creatively invented ways to access salvation and to justify himself by his own schemes, some religious and some secular. God's grace and his unconditional love have been extremely difficult for man to accept. How do I accept such amazing grace when every aspect of my justification, conversion, and transformation has nothing to do with me, but all with God? God's unconditional love and his amazing grace run counter to the core nature of man. Men and women enjoy assurances, guarantees, and warranties, which may lead us to believe that our best efforts justify us before a righteous God. Some work for salvation and exert great effort to obtain favor with God.

The Bible says in I Corinthians 13, that some give gifts to the poor, some perform great beneficial works, and some will go as far as to allow themselves to be martyred, burned at the stakes, but without Christ in the center, it means absolutely nothing.

The crux of the Gospel of Jesus Christ is salvation through faith in Jesus Christ. The Son of God has already made the ultimate sacrifice for our sins. The sacrifice was made with His own blood, which ironically should have been paid by you and me. Without requesting a payment from us, God gave us something we could neither afford nor deserve. Ephesians 2:8-9 says, *"For by grace are ye saved through faith; and that not of yourselves: it is the gift of God, not of works, lest any man should boast."* Notice that grace, unmerited favor, is given by God to show his unconditional love for mankind.

Man had no part in providing salvation, and to emphasize that no assistance is expected from man, the apostle Paul says that salvation is by grace, and not of ourselves; not by any works. He says it is a gift. Anytime someone gives a gift, there should be no strings attached. Jesus did for us what we could not do for ourselves. He gave us the gift of salvation, with no strings attached.

Through grace, God took the fall for us through his son Jesus Christ. Now he lives inside of us, continually leading and guiding us through the Holy Spirit and helping us to walk in his will. Romans 5:7-8 says, *"For scarcely for a righteous man will one die: yet peradventure for a good man some would even dare to die. But God commendeth his love toward us, in that, while we were yet sinners, Christ died for us."* God's grace saw us in our lowest base state and said, "I love you." All our debts were paid in full. Our criminal record was expunged at Calvary. We were exonerated from the stain of sin by the blood of Jesus. God's grace saw our inner beings, sinful and vile, and said, *"I want you."* God's grace rescued us when we had no knowledge we needed to be rescued. The unmerited, undeserved favor of God came upon mankind when we were not his friends, but his enemies. He paid the ultimate price.

Yes, our debt is *paid in full,* our slate wiped clean. This act of love is unparalleled throughout all of history and is truly the greatest love story of all time. And think about it, it includes you and me. Praise God!

The Gospel Message of Jesus Christ

"For I am not ashamed of the Gospel of Christ: for it is the power of God unto salvation to every one that believeth;" Romans 1:16 & 17. The Gospel is the power of God unto salvation. It is defined as *"Good News."* It is that which leads to and brings salvation. The Gospel is the power of God unto salvation to everyone that *believes.* John 3:16 says, *"For God so loved the world, that he gave his only begotten Son, that whosoever believeth in him should not perish, but have everlasting life."* It is good news that when we were all sinners headed for destruction, with no hope for rescue or salvation, God in his mercy sent his son Jesus, and wrapped him in the flesh of man and stopped our free-fall of death. Because Jesus went to the cross of Calvary and shed his precious blood for our sins, we now can have freedom and liberty from the sin, shame, and torment of separation

from God.

The sins of mankind were many and horrid, sins of thoughts, words, actions, and inaction, yet Jesus died for them all. Jesus gave the ultimate sacrifice, himself, for our sins in the past, sins in the present, and sins in the future. Heretofore, the sacrifices of bulls, goats, and lambs, atoned for sins. The blood of these animals was an accepted expiation for sins. This method of atonement was accepted under the law in the Old Testament. Yet God had a plan to unyoke man from the law by sending his son Jesus to pay the debt of sin once and for all. Hebrews 9:12 says, *"Neither by the blood of goats and calves, but by his own blood he entered in once into the Holy Place, having obtained eternal redemption for us."* There is no greater expression of love than when Christ died for mankind.

There was no good that we had done or could ever do in order to be justified in his sight or merit this great love. God had foreknowledge of our propensity to sin and to fail.

Knowing we would be as an unfaithful and promiscuous bride, Jesus still died for our sins. What type of incredible love is this, and such amazing grace, that very God would forgive us, call us his children, and make us a part of his family? (I John 3:1). This is the good news, the Gospel of salvation. God provided his son Jesus as our ultimate sacrifice in blood, paying our fare, taking our punishment, lifting our penalty, doing for us what we could not do for ourselves. This is the Gospel, the good news, the great news, that sets us free from the bondage of sin.

The Gospel in Operation

I Corinthians 15:1-4 says, "*Moreover, brethren, I declare unto you the Gospel which I preached unto you, which also ye have received, and wherein ye stand; 2) By which also ye are saved, if you keep in memory what I preached unto you, unless ye have believed in vain. 3) For I delivered unto you first of all that which I also received, how that Christ died for our sins according to the scripture; 4) And that He was buried, and that He rose again the third day according to the scriptures."*

In this passage, Paul says to the Corinthians, *"you received the Gospel and now you stand in the Gospel."* Salvation is based upon the Gospel. It is because of this good news that we are saved, freed, and redeemed. The Gospel of Jesus Christ is what transforms our spirits, renews our minds, and gives us a clean and changed heart. It is because of the Gospel, the good news, the cross of Calvary, and the blood of Jesus that we no longer have to plead guilty to sin. Because of the blood of Jesus, all of our sins are remitted and taken away. When we accept Christ, each and every one of our sins is forgiven.

Despite all sinful acts, words, or thoughts done in the past, God promises to remember them no more (Hebrews 10:17). Those acts and thoughts of incredible wickedness of which we were once partakers, are now history. By accepting the Gospel by faith, we are spiritually washed in the blood that Jesus shed at Calvary.

Actor Mel Gibson produced a movie called *The Passion of the Christ* in which he depicted the suffering of our Lord Jesus Christ. This was one of the first major movies to graphically describe the ignominious and horrible suffering and death of our Savior. However, even this movie could not completely capture what Jesus did for you and me. Jesus being stripped completely naked could not have been shown. His face and body being marred or disfigured more than any man's, (Isaiah 52:14) would have been too graphically horrific to view. Jesus endured all of that for you and for me.

Those beatings would have killed a human, and mere mortal man, but this was the Son of God hanging on that cross and man had no power over him.

All of the blood could have bled out of his body, all of the air seeped out of his lungs, all of his organs could have shut down, yet his body would have been filled with life and vigor as he gave himself as a ransom for your sins and my sins.

The great suffering at the cross of Calvary absolved mankind of any necessity to provide salvation on his own. Jesus paid it all! When we accept the Gospel, it changes hearts, cleanses minds, rinses spirits, and gives mankind a royal standing with God that is unmerited.

Because of the good news of what Jesus did at Calvary, when we accept him our sins are forgiven, our minds miraculously transformed, and our hearts changed.

Man does not have the capacity to forgive sins, transform minds, and change hearts, so God did it. There is nothing that man can add to what Jesus did. All works that men do, such as joining a church, attending service on the Sabbath, good deeds, moral living or water baptism do not save. Salvation is based on nothing that we have or could have done. It is based on what Christ has already done at Calvary.

The Gospel is the only means whereby a person can be transformed from death unto life. The Gospel, the good news of Christ dying for our sins, is God's way of showing us the ultimate act of love, sacrifice, and redemption. The life of Christ was too humble for most of mankind, so man attempts to create religions that put their savior in the most heroic light, in the most courageous and positive of positions. But Jesus came lowly, riding into Jerusalem on the back of an ass instead of a white horse.

Man has been unrelenting in exploring ways to add to what Christ has done at Calvary. Surely it cannot be that simple. Certainly there must be something man must do to augment Calvary, a work that must be done, a rule that must be kept, a regulation that must be observed, to show that we have earned salvation.

My brothers and sisters, resist the temptation to improve on what God has done. Refuse to give in to the appeal of self-atonement through works. It is against God and, in effect, nullifies all that the cross stands for. Stand firm on what Christ has done for you at Calvary. Accept this humble way, and live eternally with the Kings of all kings and the Lord of all lords.

CHAPTER NINE

Understanding Key Scripture

References

The following are scriptures commonly used to support salvation through works, specifically water baptism in Jesus' name. This section is supported by scripture reference and can be used to clarify one's belief and defend a sound biblical perspective.

I. Acts 2:38- Baptism in the Name of Jesus

Acts 2:38 is a scripture that is commonly misunderstood, and sometimes purposely used to validate erroneous teachings of baptismal regeneration.

This passage refers to events after the Holy Ghost had fallen on the day of Pentecost. Peter was preaching here and they had spoken in tongues.

Acts 2:37-38 says, *"Now when they heard this, they were pricked in their heart, and said unto Peter and to the rest of the apostles, men and brethren, what shall we do? 38) Then Peter said unto them, repent, and be baptized every one of you in the name of Jesus Christ for the remission of sins, and ye shall receive the gift of the Holy Ghost.*" The misinterpretation of this verse very often results in individuals believing that this verse reflects the direction in which they should look for the remission of sins. According to this erroneous doctrine, Peter was looking forward to water baptism to gain remission from sin.

When Peter spoke to the masses in Acts 2:38, he was speaking to an international setting of men and women (Verses 7 thru 11). These men and women had descended from all over the world with diverse customs and cultures, variegated religions, speaking many languages and dialects. Peter's mandate for baptism was not for redemption but a command to reject historic religious customs and practices, and identify with the new birth symbolized by public baptism in water. He told them to repent or turn away from past practices and accept the Christ of Calvary into their hearts. Then he instructed them to publicly be baptized as a graphic pictorial (death, burial, and resurrection) that their sins had been remitted.

Peter's command was tantamount to a convert from Islam, who has accepted Christ, being commanded to publicly show his or her acceptance of Christ and rejection of Islam by being submerged in water baptism. This would be purely spiritual symbolism, but it has grave significance. In the last days, many terrorism groups' particularly radical Islamic groups will demand public confessions and conversions to their faith under threat of death. And while there will be a greater emphasis on public confessions and various baptismal conversions worldwide, we are still only saved by grace and not of works.

As I have stated, many religious people assumed that water baptism is that which gains remission or removal of sins, but the word of God fiercely contradicts this. Baptism does not look forward to the remission of sins. Baptism looks back at the fact that remission of sins has already been gained through the blood of Christ. Baptism only symbolizes and celebrates that fact.

How is sin remitted if water baptism does not remit it? St. Matthew 26:26 shows where remission of sins comes from. The setting is the Passover, and not only the Passover, but the Lord's Last Supper. It says, *"And as they were eating, Jesus took bread, and blessed it, and brake it, and gave it to the disciples, and said, take, eat; this is my body. 27) And he took the cup, and gave thanks, and gave it to them, saying, drink ye all of it; 28) For this is my blood of the New Testament, which is shed for many for the remission of sins."* Now if you'll notice he didn't say baptism. He said, "This is my blood which is shed for many for the re-mission of sins." The word "remission" means the forgiveness, pardon, cancellation, or the release of any penalty.

He didn't say baptism gains remission as Acts 2:38 is often misinterpreted. The blood of Jesus alone is that which secures remission from sin. We should celebrate the blood of our Lord Jesus Christ.

When we are baptized, we celebrate what

the blood has done. It's a symbolic expression of what the blood has already accomplished. So we're not looking forward to gaining remission, we're looking back at the fact that our sins have already been remitted by what Jesus has done. We have accepted the gift. We're not trying to work our way into it by being baptized and therefore, gaining it by good works. We are simply receiving it by faith and grace.

II. Acts 10:38-43 - The Remission of Sins

Acts 10 contains another passage that shows us how and when our remission from sins has been secured. Certainly our salvation was not gained at the river Jordan or in the Upper Room. It was only gained for us at Calvary through the cross. In Acts 10:38 it says, *"How God anointed Jesus of Nazareth with the Holy Ghost and with power: who went about doing good, and healing all that were oppressed of the devil; for God was with Him. 39) And we are witnesses of all things which he did both in the land of the Jews, and in Jerusalem; whom they slew and hanged on a tree: 40) Him God raised up the third day, and shewed Him open-ly; 41) Not to all the people, but unto witnesses chosen before God, even to us, who did eat and drink with Him after he rose from the dead. 42) And He commanded us to preach unto the peo-ple, and to testify that it is He which was or-dained of God to be the judge of quick and dead. 43) To Him give all the prophets witness, that through His name whosoever believeth in Him shall receive remission of sins."* So here remission is identified with believing in the Lord Jesus Christ, not being baptized. Water baptism highlights salvation; it simply illus-trates it. It is only through the blood of Jesus that you are saved.

III. Romans 3:23-28

Romans 3:23-24 says, *"For all have sinned, and come short of the glory of God; 24) Being justified freely by his grace through the redemp-tion that is in Christ Jesus:"* We are justified freely, not by works or anything that we do, but freely. Verse 25 continues, *"Whom God hath set forth to be a propitiation through faith in His blood, to declare his righteousness for the remission of sins that are past, through the forbearance of God;"* Remember you look back at the fact that remission has already been secured. Verse 26 says, *"To declare, I say, at this time His righteousness: That He might be just, and the justifier of him which believeth in Jesus. 27) Where is boasting then? It is excluded. By what law? Of works? Nay: but by the law of faith."*

In what can we boast? We cannot boast in water baptism, being faithful to our spouses, preaching to thousands or being faithful to our churches. We don't join a church to gain salvation although the Bible tells us to go to church. We go to church *because* we are saved. You don't have to go to church to get saved.

You can get saved anywhere. All one has to do is receive the free gift of Jesus. Where is boasting then? We cannot boast in the fact that we were baptized on some stormy day or on some sunshiny day. No one can boast in their good deeds, moral behavior, or clean living. These are all excluded. Verse 28 says, *"Therefore we conclude that a man is justified by faith without the deeds of the law."* We do good deeds because we *are* saved; we live holy lives because we are redeemed.

An individual receives the Purple Heart for valor above and beyond the call of duty. He receives the Medal of Honor for bravery. Was the bravery demonstrated before the decoration or after the decoration? Of course, the bravery had to be shown before the decoration and the decoration looks back at the act of bravery. So it is with remission of sins. Christ at Calvary remitted sins. An individual accepts it and then is baptized.

Once you are saved, then get baptized, be filled with the Holy Ghost, speak in tongues, walk in the Spirit, live a triumphant prosperous life, and accept all the benefits of being a Christian.

IV. I Peter 3:17-21

This is another text that is commonly inter-preted inaccurately. Read carefully now, *"For it is better, if the will of God be so, that ye suffer for well doing, than for evil doing. 18) For Christ also hath once suffered for sins, the just for the unjust, that He might bring us to God, being put to death in the flesh, but quickened by the spir-it: 19) By which also He went and preached un-to the spirits in prison; 20) Which sometime were disobedient, when once the longsuffering of God waited in the days of Noah, while the Ark was a preparing, wherein few, that is, eight souls were saved by water. 21) The like figure whereunto even baptism doth also now save us (not the putting away of the filth of the flesh, but the answer of a good conscience toward God,) by the resurrection of Jesus Christ."* The portion of Verse 20 that is commonly used in error's *"eight souls were saved by water."*

Let's go back and look at the wording care-fully. Verse 21 explicitly says that baptism is a figure. If it's a figure, it's not the substance. If it's the figure, it simply mirrors something. Verse 21 tells us at least four things about baptism:

1) It's only a figure

2) It does not put away the filth of the flesh (it doesn't save you)

3) It is the answer of a good conscience toward God

4) It does not create a good conscience (it's an expression of what has already been made good and acceptable before the Lord)

Since this text does not intimate salvation through baptism, let's see what the Apostle Paul was talking about. In Hebrews 11:7 we read, *"By faith Noah, being warned of God of things not seen as yet, moved with fear, prepared an ark to the saving of his house;"* What had he not seen yet? In I Peter 3:20 it says "saved by water" and in Verse 21 it is a figure of Noah's faith. Which came first, Noah's faith or the water? The same water that saved Noah by lifting the boat is the same water that killed everybody else. So faith came first. Faith saved his house. Noah in this example, who was never baptized in water along with many other old testament saints and is described as having a good conscience towards God despite opposition he faced constructing the ark. Noah was incredibly old (600 years old). It had never rained before. He built a three story ark on dry land and filled it with every type of animal and bird. He had a massive storage of food, and for 120 years invited people into the ark for safety. Noah's faith in God was rewarded through the saving of his family in the ark. Water baptism symbolizes a life wiped clean through the blood of Jesus, just as sinful earth was wiped clean through the flood.

To clarify salvation through Jesus' blood, Peter says at the end of verse 21, *"by the resurrection of Jesus Christ."* Verses 20 and 21 develop earlier passages of scripture, particularly verses 13-17 where Peter is teaching to stand for Christ despite the repercussions or outcomes. Noah was an excellent example as the

Bible says in II Timothy 3:16, *"All scripture is given by inspiration of God, and is profitable for doctrine, for reproof, for correction, for instruction in righteousness."* Noah I'm sure was laughed to scorn, he would have been mocked on late night television, called a fanatic, and alienated. For a first-century Christian, being baptized in water identified that person with Christ and also made it difficult for that person to renege on their personal commitment since they had publicly acknowledged their faith. The Apostle Peter never taught salvation through water baptism and I Peter 1:3-5 says, *"Blessed be the God and Father of our Lord Jesus, which according to his abundant mercy hath begotten us again unto a lively hope by the resurrection of Jesus Christ from the dead, 4) To an inheritance incorruptible, and undefiled, and that fadeth not away, reserved in heaven for you, 5) Who are kept by the power of God through faith unto salvation read to be revealed in the last time."*

V. Hebrews 10:22

In Hebrews 10:22 it says, *"Let us draw near with a true heart in full assurance of faith, having our hearts sprinkled from an evil conscience, and our bodies washed with pure water."* This is another scripture often misinterpreted and taken out of context. The pure water referred to here is symbolism of the Word of the Lord. It is clearly not speaking of baptism because the waters of baptism are not pure or clean. It is not referring here to literal water because we know as pure as any company has tried to make it, water is not 100% pure of particles and molecules. The pure water referred to here is symbolism of the Word of the Lord. It symbolizes the washing that comes by the Word. For example, the scripture says in I John 1:7, *"But if we walk in the light, as he is in the light, we have fellowship one with another, and the blood of Jesus Christ his Son cleanseth us from all sin."*

The Bible illuminates this further in Ephesians 5:26 when it says,*"That he might sanctify and cleanse it with the washing of the water by the word..."* Christ's death enabled the church to become that holy bride set apart for himself. This cleansing takes place by the preaching of God's Word, that washes us, cleanses us, and rinses us, making us to shine the radiant light of Christ. This is not referring to any baptismal regeneration doctrine, as the Apostle Paul strongly taught against salvation by works. Paul said to Titus in Titus 3:5-7 *"Not by works of righteousness which we have done, but according to his mercy he saved us, by the washing of regeneration, and renewing of the Holy Ghost; 6) Which he shed on us abundantly through Jesus Christ our Savior; 7) That being justified by his grace, we should be made heirs according to the hope of eternal life."* We are not justified, redeemed, or transformed by water but by the blood of Jesus.

While I enjoy the praise and worship music of this generation, as I'm heading toward my 80th birthday, my heart longs for the old songs that spoke of the struggles God brought me through, songs about heaven and the blood of Jesus, old songs like *"Jesus paid it all. All to Him I owe. Sin had left a crimson stain, but Jesus blood washed it whiter than snow."*

Beloved children, accept Christ for who He is and what He has done. Nothing else needs to be added to what Christ has already done to redeem our salvation. Accept Him today, right now. Reject the past; we all have one. Jesus is the only one who never needed an eraser or needed to apologize. We all need forgiveness and transformed lives that only God can give through the blood of Jesus.

All you have to do is accept Jesus as your Lord and Savior Jesus Christ and turn away from sins, religious and civic works and behaviors and anything else that is contrary to the Word of God. The call goes out, please accept Him today. You will find that God's way is the only way that leads to eternal life, peace and happiness.

VI. Ephesians 4:5 One Lord, One Faith, One Baptism

One Lord, one faith, one baptism is one of the most divisively misused scriptures used to support works based on salvation. This verse is used to intimidate Christians into doing something against scripture and the cross of Calvary, and that is accept water baptism as the means through which a regenerated life comes. Don't be fooled. As has been stated earlier in this book, there were a number of terms used when referring to water baptism in the book of Acts. Jesus gave the only specific formula in scripture for the ritual of water baptism (St. Matthew 28:19-20). However, this scripture in Ephesians 4:5 has absolutely nothing to do with water baptismal salvation. This scripture speaks of the spiritual baptism that takes place through faith at the point of conversion to Christ.

The Bible says in I Corinthians 12:13, *"For by one Spirit are we all baptized into one body, whether we be Jews or Gentiles, whether we be bond or free; and have been all made to drink into one Spirit."* When a person receives Christ in his or her heart through faith, the Holy Spirit of God places or baptizes that person into the body of Christ. They are at that point, the point of acceptance of what Christ has done at Calvary, united and identified with him. They can do nothing further to seal their relationship with God. Jesus told the thief (an unbaptized believer) on the cross in St. Luke 23:43, *"This day thou shalt be with me in paradise."* At the point of acceptance of Christ, that man was saved, set free from sins, and placed into the body of Christ. Praise God for the precious blood of Jesus!

Once the spiritual conversion takes place, all sins are forgiven, and your spirit is transformed from darkness to the newness of light. Regarding water baptism, whether administered immediately after this, 30 to 90 days later, or whenever, is only a witness to what you have done and graphically pictures the spiritual conversion that took place.

Paul taught the church at Ephesus, a church sometimes divided by culture and tradition, that we are all one body in Christ. One Lord, our Savior Jesus Christ the Son of God; one faith, we have a common faith in Christ, are all trusting in Jesus Christ for salvation; and finally one baptism, we're all baptized by the Holy Spirit into the same body of Christ. This verse, Ephesians 4:5 is used to hoodwink and bamboozle people into thinking they can help Jesus out in salvation. It was never meant to "scare" local churches into baptizing one way; with water, fully immersed in "Jesus' Name" emerging speaking in tongues or else. I cannot emphasize this enough; water baptism of any kind under any format or formula of names cannot wash away sins or save you.

In Galatians 3:26-28, Paul writes a similar theme of unity, *"For ye are all the children of God by faith in Christ Jesus. 27) For as many of you as have been baptized into Christ have put on Christ. 28) There is neither Jew nor Greek, there is neither bond nor free, there is neither male or female: for ye are all one in Christ Jesus.*" Note how Paul emphasizes the unity of the body of Christ by referring to the Holy Spirit placing or baptizing all believers into the body of Christ. <u>Every time the word baptism is used in scripture it does not refer to water and every time water is used it does not refer to baptism.</u> The spiritual baptism is what only the Holy Spirt can do, (I Corinthians12:13) which is how one is placed into the body of Christ. Paul certainly never taught regeneration through water baptism performed by man. Paul clearly taught that water baptism is an outward showing for others, of what has taken place on the inside by Christ. Ephesians 2:8-9 says, *"by grace are ye saved through faith; and that not of yourselves; it is the gift of God: Not of works, lest any man should boast."*

Little children, Jesus Christ is all you need, the lowly message of the cross, that Jesus is the Son of God, sent down in the form of a man to suffer, carry our sins, and then die so that we can have a right to the tree of life. Accept what Christ has done for you, it's simple; it's plain, unsophisticated and humble but will save your soul from sin and hell. I Corinthians 1:27-31 says, *"But God hath chosen the foolish things of the world to confound the wise; and God hath chosen the weak things of the world to confound the things which are mighty; 28) And base things of the world, and things which are despised, hath God chosen, yea, and things which are not, to bring to nought things that are: 28) That no flesh should glory in his presence. 30) But of him are ye in Christ Jesus, who of God is made unto us wisdom, and righteousness, and sanctification, and redemption: 31) That, according as it is written, He that glorieth, let him glory in the Lord."* Our redemption is in Christ Jesus only, as base, ignorant and foolish as they may seem to some. The Bible says in Romans 1:16, *"...that the Gospel of Jesus Christ is the power of God unto salvation to everyone that believeth."* It has the power to save your soul, wash you from sins, redeem your life from destruction, cleanse your mind and spirit and have you in right standing with God through the blood of Jesus. The Bible says in St. John 14:6, *"Jesus saith unto him, I am the way, the truth, and the life: no man cometh unto the Father, but by me."* Little children no one gets to the Father through works of any kind, not through Mother Mary, angels, or any other route other than the cross of Calvary

I ask that you accept what Christ Jesus has already done for you, be ready to meet Him in death or in the rapture not based on what you have done, but based on what Jesus accomplished at Calvary. Remember, it's not what we do that saves us, but what Christ has done. All He asks us to do is accept it by faith.

CHAPTER TEN

Salvation through Christ Jesus

There is nothing that can save you but the blood of Jesus. Your salvation has already been provided. There is nothing you can do to help provide your salvation. When scriptures are misinterpreted to state that water baptism is necessary to obtain salvation, it is a serious misreading.

The Bible doesn't talk about adding names to the Book of Life. It only talks about God blotting out names from the Book of Life (Revelation 3:15). Why? Because when an individual is born, God puts everybody's name in the Book of Life. Everybody! The assumption is that God has made a provision for the salvation of all mankind. The scripture declares that it is not God's will that any should perish (II Peter 3:9). Therefore, God has already placed everybody's name in the Book of Life. He's letting you know that there is a nameplate on God's table of abundance for everybody, including you. He's already made provision for your eternal life with Christ. Praise God! All you have to do is accept it. The only time a person's nameplate is removed is if that person dies outside of God or if that person is depending on what he or she has done, their good works, or walking in sin and refusing to accept Jesus as Savior, Lord, and Master.

Jesus said, *"Come unto me all ye that labor and are heavy laden and I will give you rest."* (Matthew 11:28-29). There is no other Savior, but the Lord Jesus Christ. If you become a disciple of any other god other than the true and living God and you die in your sins, you will go to hell. Salvation is not in Confucius or Buddha. It's not in Hinduism, Shintoism, or Animism. It's not in any of these. Salvation is only in Jesus Christ. One of the boldest, baddest, most powerful statements ever recorded in history is found in St. John 14:6, when Jesus said *"I am the Way, the Truth, and the Life: no man cometh unto the Father, but by Me."* This means the only road leading to real truth and eternal life comes from Jesus and the way to God the Father is only through Jesus Christ the Son. Yes little children salvation is only through Jesus' blood, which was shed at Calvary. Water baptism could never do it and should never be put on the same level as the precious blood of Jesus. It is an affront and a ridiculous outrage to draw any comparison between the transforming blood being shed at Calvary and an individual being dipped in a pool filled with water!

Look at Hebrews 9:11-12 which says, *"But Christ being come an High Priest of good things to come, by a greater and more perfect tabernacle, not made with hands, that is to say, not of this building; 12) neither by the blood of goats and calves, but by his own blood he entered in once into the holy place, having obtained eternal redemption for us."* There's nothing we can do to add to it. Hebrews 10:9-10 says: *"Then said he, Lo, I come to do thy will, O God. He taketh away the first, that he may establish the second. 10) By the which will we are sanctified through the offering of the body of Jesus Christ once for all."* It's already done. Nothing else can be done. Verse 11 continues, *"And every priest standeth daily ministering and offering often-times the same sacrifices, which can never take away sins: 12) But this man, after he had of-fered one sacrifice for sins for ever, sat down on the right hand of* God; 13) *From henceforth ex-pecting till his enemies be made his footstool. 14) For by one offering he hath perfected for ev-er them that are sanctified."*

Right now Jesus is on the right hand of the Father and He offered himself once. Redemption has already been secured.

Hebrews 10:16 says, *"This is the covenant that I will make with them after those days, saith the Lord, I will put my laws into their heart, and in their minds will I write them; 17) and their sins and iniquities will I remember no more. 18) Now where remission of these is, there is no more offering for sin."* Our sins have al-ready been remitted. That's what the writer of Hebrews is telling us. This man Jesus has al-ready offered himself once for our sins. It's al-ready been done. Verse 19 says, *"Having there-fore, brethren, boldness to enter into the holiest by the blood of Jesus,"* The only thing we can do now is to enter into the holiest by the blood of Jesus.

The good news is that Jesus paid it all. He covered all our sin debts. The son of the living God died for all of our sins. He paid the ultimate price and gave the supreme sacrifice for your redemption. God has good things in store for those who walk by faith in what he has done and not by what mankind attempts to do through water baptism. I know I have been redundant in this book, but I'd rather be redundant if it clarifies the scripture for someone, gives a scriptural defense for their faith, pulls someone into heaven, saves a soul from hell or causes someone to put their trust solely in what Christ has done on Calvary.

CHAPTER ELEVEN

How to Receive Jesus Christ as Your Lord and Savior

I ask that you now consider the most important decision of your life, accepting Jesus Christ as your personal Savior. What do you need to do? God made salvation plain and simple so everyone born could receive it. All you have to do is accept what Christ has already done for you. Ask Jesus into your heart. Romans 10:9-10 says, *"That if thou shalt confess with thy mouth the Lord Jesus, and shalt believe in thy heart that God hath raised him from the dead, thou shalt be saved. For with the heart man believeth unto righteousness; and with the mouth confession is made unto salvation."* Confess with your mouth that Jesus is the Christ, the Anointed One, and believe in your innermost being that God raised Jesus from the dead, you will be saved. Again, you are saved by the grace of God through your faith in him and what he has done (Ephesians 2:8-9). That's it! The salvation of God is truly amazing, we couldn't earn it, we don't deserve it, and God was the only one who could provide it. Thank God for His incredible gift of salvation.

Romans 3:23 says, *"All have sinned and come short before the glory of God."* We are all born into sin, and every person on the face of the earth needs Jesus to pardon our sins. Romans 6:23 says, *"For the wages of sin is death; but the gift of God is eternal life through Jesus Christ our Lord."* Because of sin, what awaited us was death and ultimately eternal suffering in the lake of fire, burning with literal fire and brimstone (Revelation 21:8). Yet, because of the great love that God has for us, He sent his only begotten Son, who had never known sin, to die on a criminals cross for you and I. St. John 3:16 says, *"For God so loved the world, that he gave his only begotten Son, that whosoever believeth in him should not perish, but have everlasting life."*

My son, my daughter, believe what God has already done for you. If you are religious and thought you were saved based on water baptism, joining a church, passing out literature on Saturday mornings, being a good person, doing good deeds, pray this prayer with me:

Dear Lord Jesus, I believe that you died on the cross for my sins and that you rose again on the third day. I confess that I'm a sinner and accept what you have accomplished at Calvary to take away my sins through the blood of Jesus. Forgive me of all my sins Lord Jesus, as I denounce any work that I have done that exalts itself against the cross of Calvary and what you have already provided through your blood. Wash me and make me clean, in Jesus' name, amen.

At that point my son and daughter, you will be saved. You may not feel the splash of water, a tingling down the spine, the joyous applause of men, a ceremonious announcement, but by faith, you are saved.

Once you've accepted Christ and your sins have been pardoned, by all means join a church, sign up to be baptized in water, attend church regularly, pass out Christian literature to your friends and loved ones, live a holy and clean life, express the love and joy of God to all you come in contact with. Once you've accepted Christ, His blood will wash away your sins, habits, or addictions. Allow the Holy Spirit to give you power over immoral thoughts and behaviors. Man and medication can only go so far, but God can deliver completely from depression, deep hurts and wounds, bitterness, unforgiveness, worry, disobedience, self-righteousness, stubbornness and rebellion and all manner of evil. He's a loving God ready to deliver from homosexuality, lesbianism, adultery, fornication, masturbation, pornography, and all other sexual sins and abundantly pardon and graciously forgive you! What amazing grace from an amazing God. He loves you just the way you are and wants you just the way you are, because he alone has provided a way of salvation and change, a new birth and a transformed life for you (Romans 12:1-2). God has promised to give you joy and peace, He will fill your heart with love and forgiveness, He will take away anxiety, and lack of self-respect, self-worth, and fill you with the fruit of His Holy Spirit; love, joy, peace, longsuffering, gentleness, goodness, faith, meekness, temperance, against such there is no law, rule or regulation that can stop a Christian from exhibiting these characteristics (Galatians 5:22).

Little children, accept Jesus now, don't delay and don't wait. Today is the day of salvation for you. Jesus is calling you to make that decision in a hurry. Tomorrow is not promised for me, you, or anyone else. Today is all we have to work with. So, I pray that you allow the Savior of the world to become the Lord of your life. Amen.

CHAPTER TWELVE

What's Next for the Earth

The next big event that will take place on the earth according to the Bible is the coming of the Lord Jesus, commonly called, "the rapture of the church." This is that great "Catching Away" that will happen to all those who have accepted Christ as their personal Savior and have been washed in the blood of the lamb. This is what every Saint of God should be actively looking for. The coming of the Lord is closer than we all realize and I want you and all of your loved ones to be ready. I Thessalonians 4:16-18 says, *"For the Lord himself shall descend from heaven with a shout, with the voice of the archangel, and with the trump of God: and the dead in Christ shall rise first: 17) Then we which are alive and remain shall be caught up together with them in the clouds, to meet the Lord in the air and so shall we ever be with the Lord. 18) Wherefore comfort one another with these words."* Jesus is coming for those who have been washed in His blood and will spare us just like the Lord spared all those who put the blood of a lamb on their lintels and side posts in Exodus 12:23. We won't be caught away with Him in the rapture because of anything we've done or said, but because of the precious blood of Jesus.

The Bible tells us that Jesus will come for us like a thief in the night (I Thessalonians 5:2) in the sense that no one knows the exact day or hour (St. Matthew 24:36). Yet the Bible gives us a clear description of what times will be like all over the world prior to His coming. II Timothy 3:1-5 lets us know that in the last days perilous or dangerous times would come. We're living in those dangerous days of rampant murder, escalading terrorism, mass killings in our schools, malls, and many places of large gatherings. In that same passage of scripture it also lets us know that the last days would be defined by people *"having a form of godliness, but denying the power thereof and for you not to agree with them."*

These are religious folk. There are many good church going people who live exemplary lives but are outside the ark of safety because they are denying the power of God through the blood of Jesus. They act like, walk like, talk like, sing like, preach like, pray like, worship like, but they are not like Christ. They only have the form, the style, and Paul tells Timothy in verse 3:5, *"from such turn away."* Paul says to take this serious, if they refuse to accept what Christ has done, get away from them. The scripture that says if another gospel is preached it is a curse. In Galatians 1:6-8, it says, 6) *I am amazed that you are so quickly turning away from Him who called you by the grace of Christ, and are turning to a different gospel 7) not that there is another gospel, but there are some who are troubling you and want to change the gospel of Christ. 8) But even if we or an angel from heaven should preach to you a gospel other than what we have preached to you a curse be on him!*

Some of the major preachers in America, refuse to accept regeneration solely and exclusively through the blood of Jesus. They believe that self-effort or prosperity plays a role in a transformed life. Paul says to be aware of this in the last days, and regardless of how inspiring their sermons, how powerful their messages, how large their churches, if the cross is not the core of their message, *"From such turn away."* (II Timothy 3:5) Preacher man, preacher woman, pastor, bishop, apostle, deacon, choir member, church member, non-church member or sinner, we all need to be saved through the blood of Jesus.

Little children, the time is short, II Thessalonians 3:13 says, *"But ye, brethren, be not weary in well doing."* Be about our Father's business, pray that God would send a last day move of God to America and the world before He comes. A revival and harvest where men and women are saved by the grace of God and empowered by the Holy Ghost and are telling everyone they know that Jesus is alive, and well, and ready to forgive sins, and He is coming again soon. I Thessalonians 5:9, *"For God hath not appointed us to wrath, but to obtain salvation by our Lord Jesus Christ."* God has not appointed us to go through the tribulation and will rapture us out of the earth before that time. Then lawlessness like you've never seen will take place on the earth. Once the Holy Ghost comes for us and His presence is no longer in the earth, the fierceness of sin will take over on a horrific level.

God forbid that anyone reading this book should be left behind. The milk and bread and meat on the shelf in the supermarkets will come at a stiff price. Don't be fooled by America's prosperity and good life so that you expect this forever. Gasoline, oil, water, clothing, and basic necessities will be accessible on condition. To make any purchases, travel, work, pay bills, or go to school, one will receive a mark of the beast on their forehead or hand, which damns that person's soul to a literal eternal hell fire (Revelation 19:20). Online purchases will be tracked, Facebook users will be tracked along with cellphone users. The time to receive Christ is right now while the Holy Ghost's presence is in the earth. My son, my daughter, turn from sin, works, rules or any doctrines not like Christ and accept the grace of God and receive Him into your heart today. He's waiting, He's willing and He's ready to receive you as his son or daughter. Believe on the Lord Jesus Christ, and not only will he save you, but your household, your loved ones as well (Acts 16:31). God loves you and everything that He's done, He's done it for you. God's love for mankind, for you is so great that He spared us and He gave up His only Son for you and me (John 3:16).

Naturally, logically or any other way, God should have protected his Son and let us get what we deserve, but grace! God's will is that you be saved and free from sin, and living eternally forever with Him. He has promised to prepare a place for you where there is no more sorrow, no more pain, no more death or sickness or terror. Let Him in today, so you too can be forever with the Lord. May you experience the grace of our Lord Jesus Christ in a new and refreshing way Amen.

ABOUT THE AUTHOR

Rev. Harold A. Arrington

Pastor Harold Arrington was the Founder and Pastor of *Bethel Gospel Tabernacle Church* in Harvey, Illinois where he served for 56 years. He was born in 1934 during the Great Depression.

Pastor Arrington was married to his lovely bride Barbara for 60 years. They have nine children, three daughters and six sons, eight grandchildren, and eight great-grandchildren and several great great-grandchildren.

Although Pastor Arrington went on to be with the Lord, his ministry is being carried out by his sons, John Arrington, Senior Pastor and Paul Arrington, Outreach Ministries Pastor.

Pastor Arrington was a hard working husband and father for his family. His greatest desire was to see all his family and loved ones enter into the kingdom of heaven.

He received a myriad of awards from organizations recognizing him as a pioneer for preaching on TV. His core vision of reaching the broken, hurting, the hungry and the lost is the reason there are many Christian programs on television across the country today. He was the first to have a Christian preaching program on television in the Chicagoland area.

During the 1970s and 1980s, he produced, directed and hosted the live television show, *Impact* on WCIU-Channel 26.

Impact was the first of its kind in the state of Illinois at that time to feature Christian television designed specifically for preaching the Word of God.

The only other shows known nationally were the *Oral Roberts* and *Billy Graham Crusades*, however, Pastor Arrington helped pave the way for preaching on cable and network TV as we know it today.

There are countless cable TV programs that cater to Christians. *Trinity Broadcasting Network (TBN), The Word Network,* and *Daystar* are a few that are piped into millions of homes every day all because of Spirit-filled pioneers like Pastor Arrington who helped pave the way for the preaching of the Word of God on cable and network TV.

Impact included testimonies of men and women who had been saved from all manner of sin through the blood of Jesus. It also included the singing of musical groups and choirs.

Today this programming is the norm on television. We praise God for the vision and foresight of Pastor Arrington.

In 1984, the Spirit of the Lord again led Pastor Arrington to create a call in for prayer radio program called *The Tabernacle Hour*, affectionately known as "America's Prayer Meeting Of The Air". The radio show was heard on FM stations WLNR 106.3 and WYCA 92.3 and their affiliates. Many people were saved, encouraged, bodies were healed, and souls delivered and set free from the powers of darkness through this ministry of prayer. It was on the air for an amazing five hours per night. *The Tabernacle Hour* ushered in many of the radio shows we hear today.

After being on the air for almost 26 years straight, Pastor Arrington decided to move on to other areas of ministry that God had led him including supporting orphanages, schools, feeding the hungry and spreading the gospel in West Africa, East Africa, and South Africa, which continues to grow and expand under his sons' today.

In 1984, after Pastor Arrington's eldest son became addicted to drugs, Pastor and Mother Arrington began to recognize the tremendous number of African-American men strung out on drugs, alcohol, other addictions, and saddled with mental problems and challenges. Pastor and Mother Arrington then started the *Page One Ministry*, which is a 13-month men's rehabilitation program for men with drug, alcohol, and street addictions, to reset the story of their lives at the first page, hence the name, 'Page One' Ministry. The goal is for 1,000 men to hear the gospel and accept the grace of God, and be discipled, educated, and trained to become men of character and courage, and productive members of society.

This program has been a lifesaver to hundreds of men of all races, creeds, and colors.

Pastor Arrington's eldest son has now accepted Christ as his personal savior and is saved by the grace of God through his faith in our Lord and savior Jesus Christ.

Those of Pastor Arrington's children currently outside of the ark of safety of grace throughout the country will one day come to know Christ personally and will live eternally in heaven with the family of God from all over the world! What a great day of rejoicing that will be!

There is no greater responsibility or reward than seeing people come into the kingdom of God. So take this Gospel of grace everywhere you can before is too late, to every city and village, to the rich and to the poor, to the good and to be bad, to everyone of every race and religion. Don't hold back this Gospel, don't sit on it, but get excited about this Gospel of grace, get up and go, take this Gospel to the ends of the Earth, so as many as possible can experience God's love, favor and grace.

Pastor & Mother Arrington